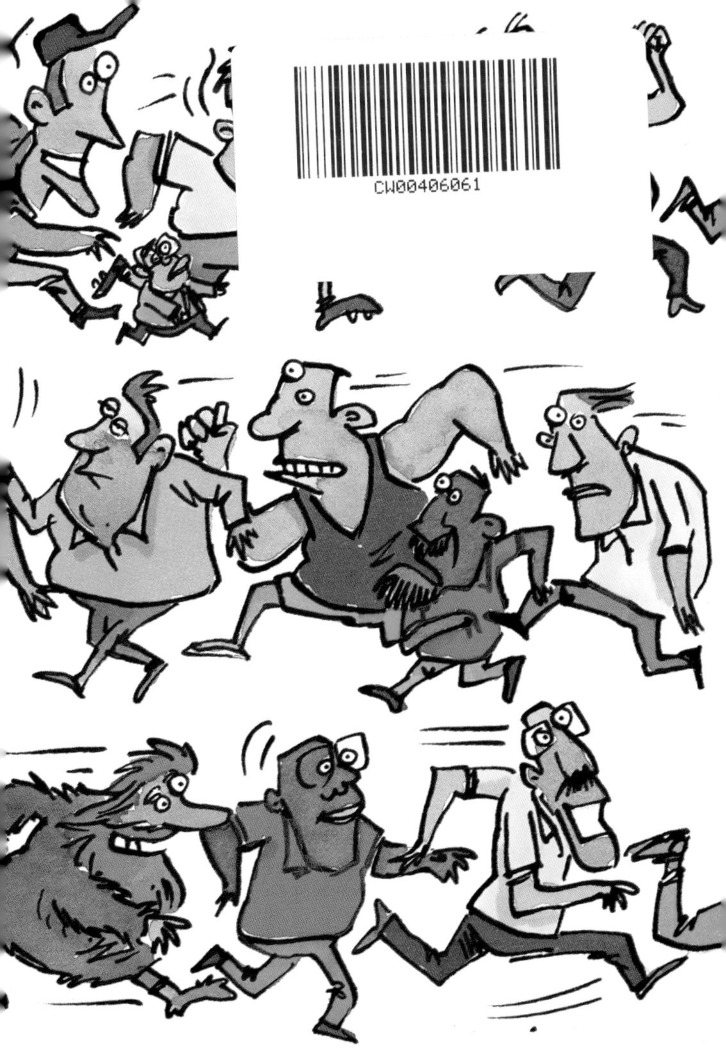

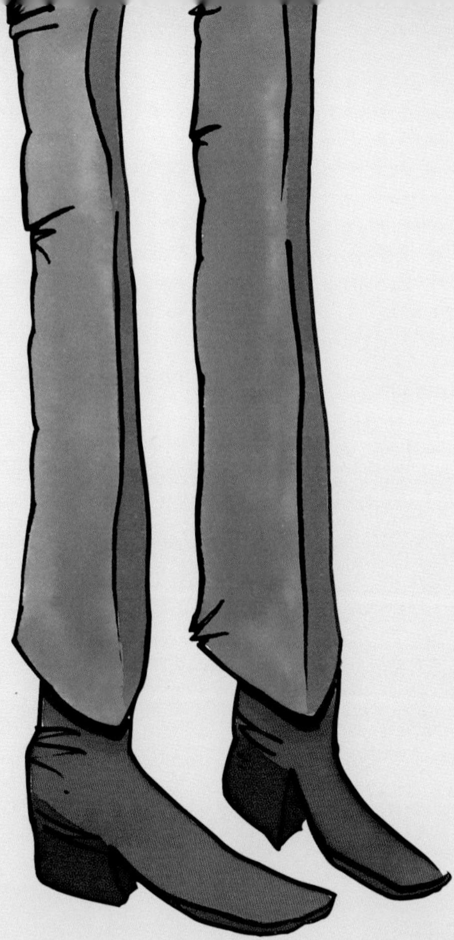

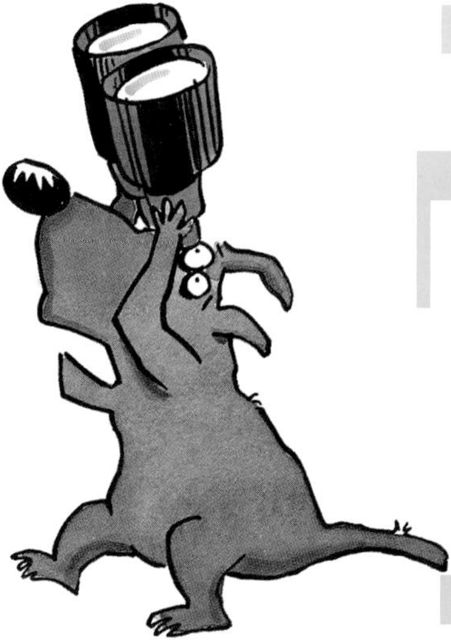

Too Tall

too little

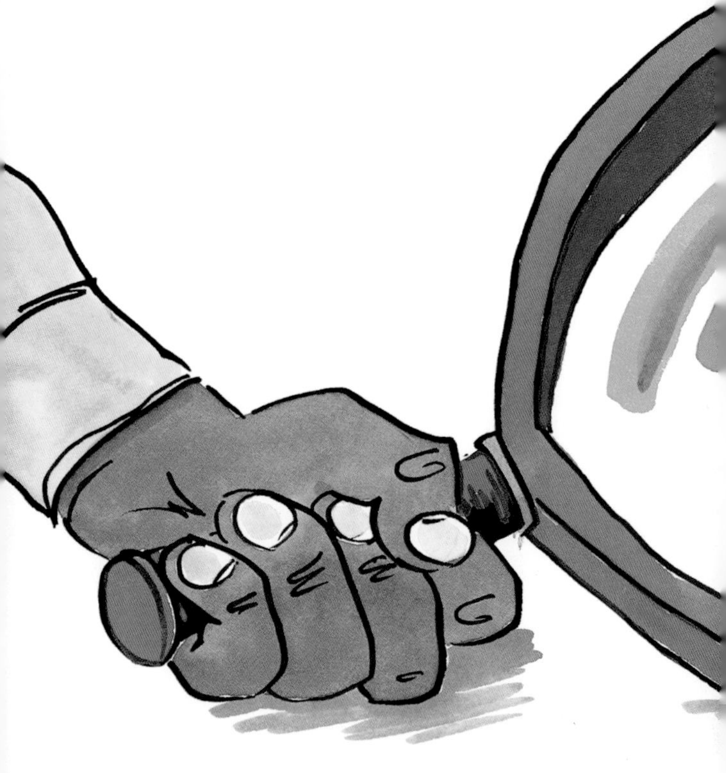

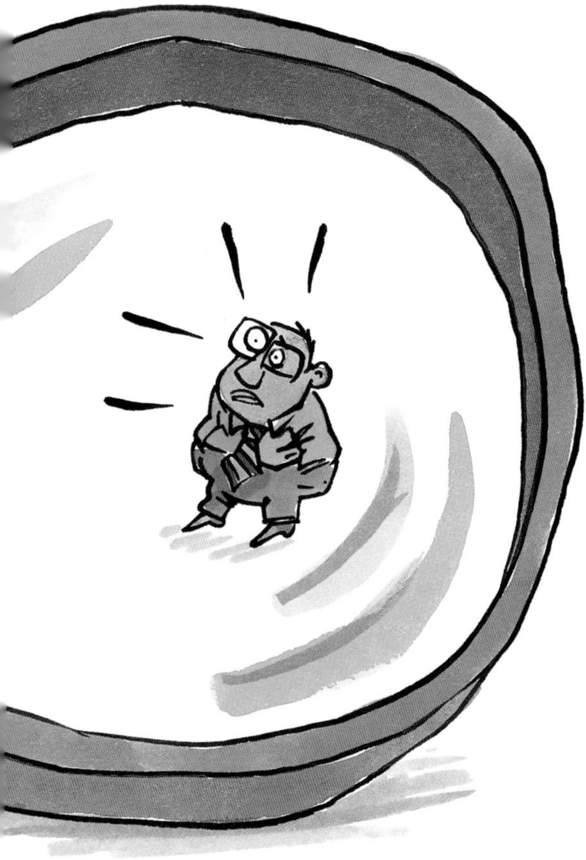

Too lazy

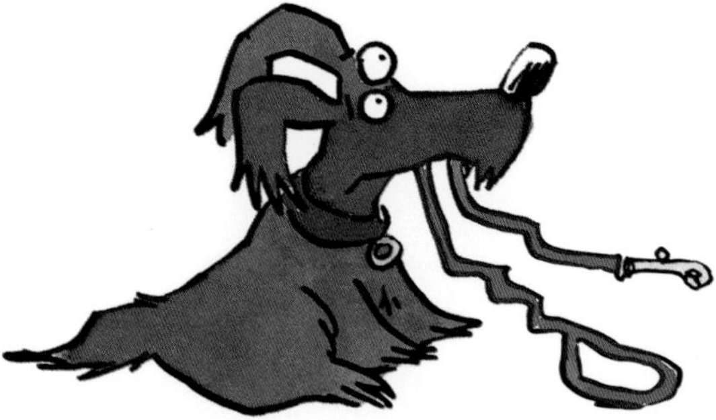

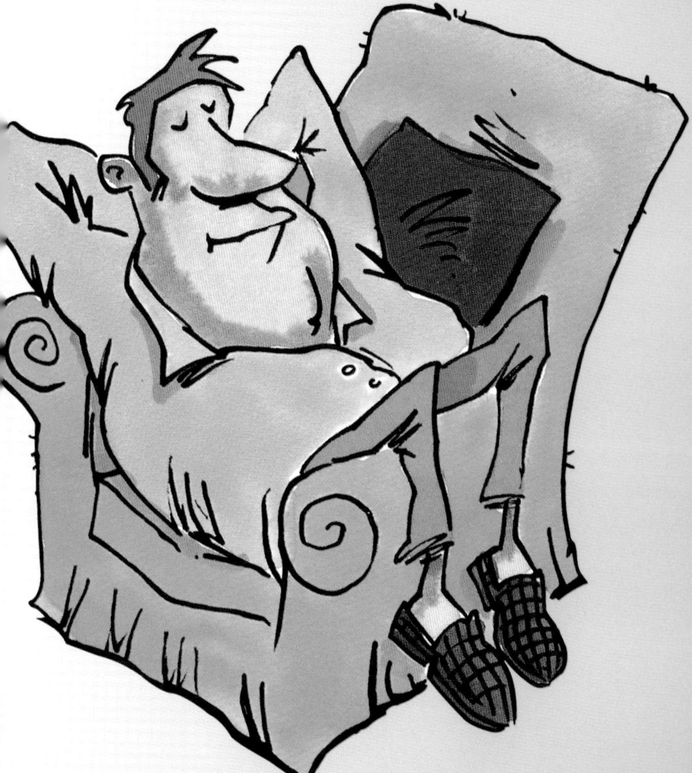

Too embarrassing . . .

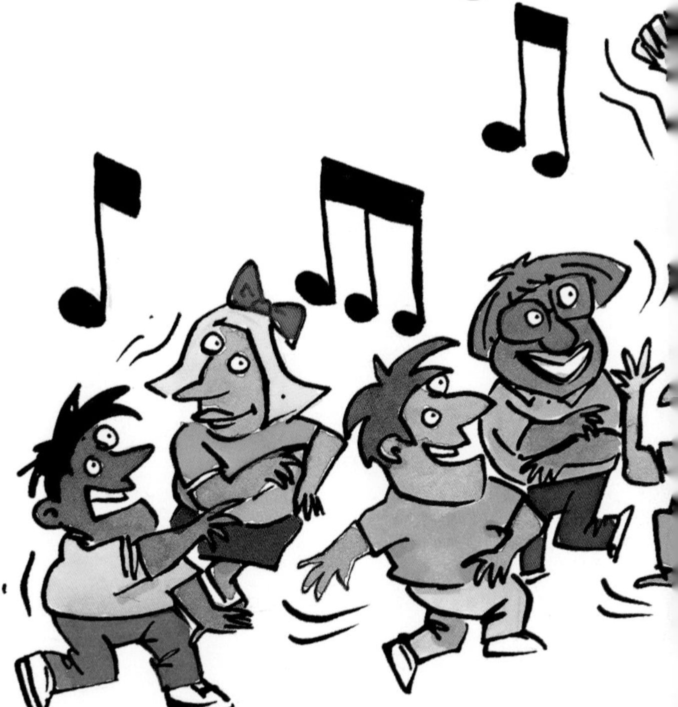

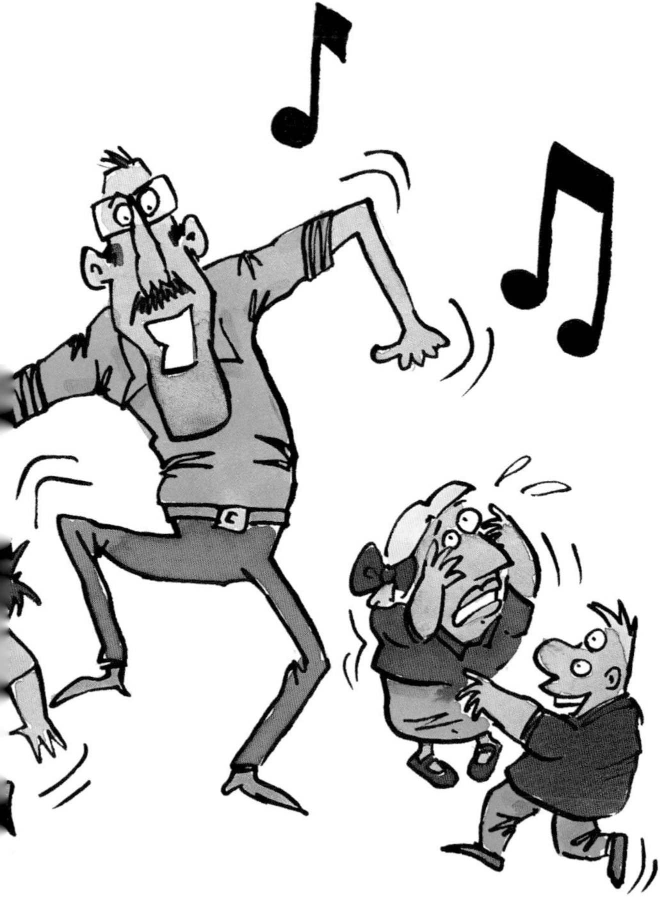

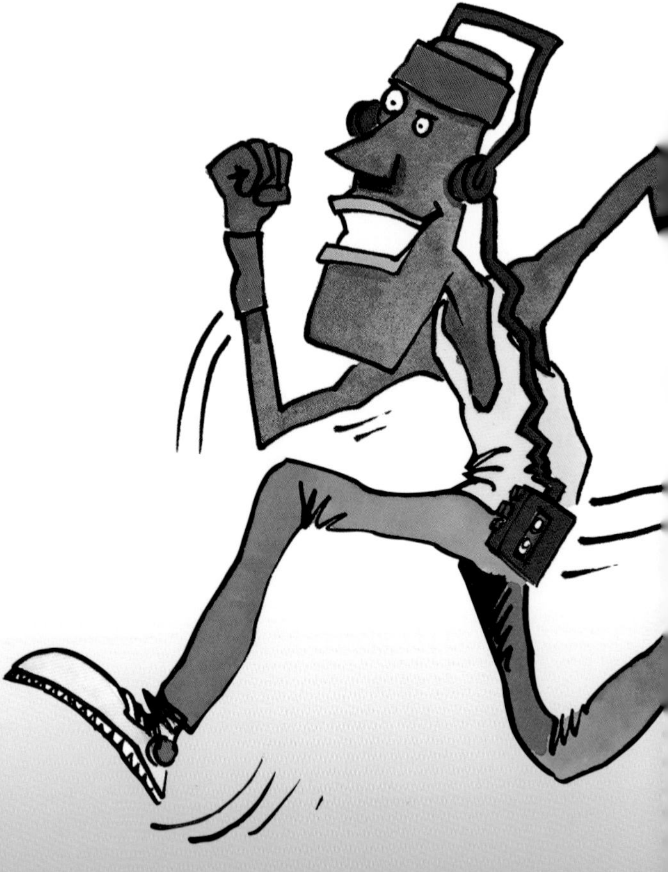

Too keen

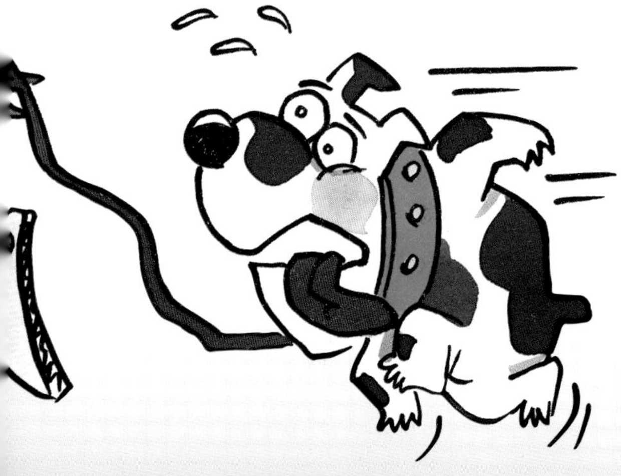

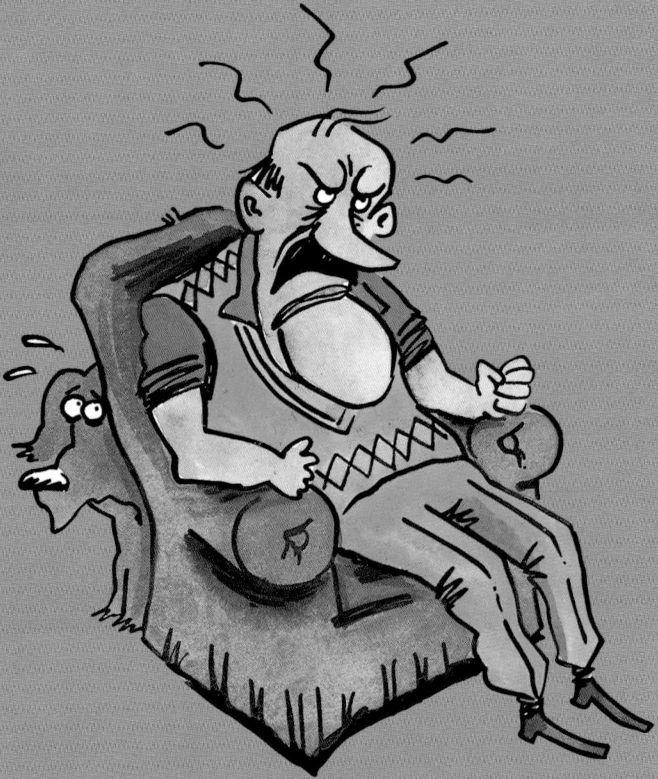

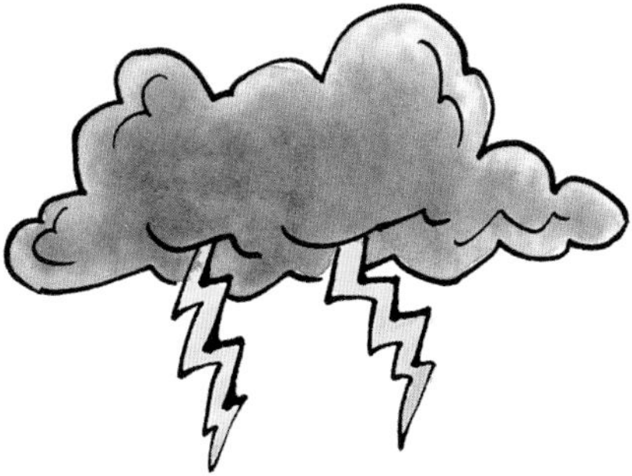

TOO GRUMPY

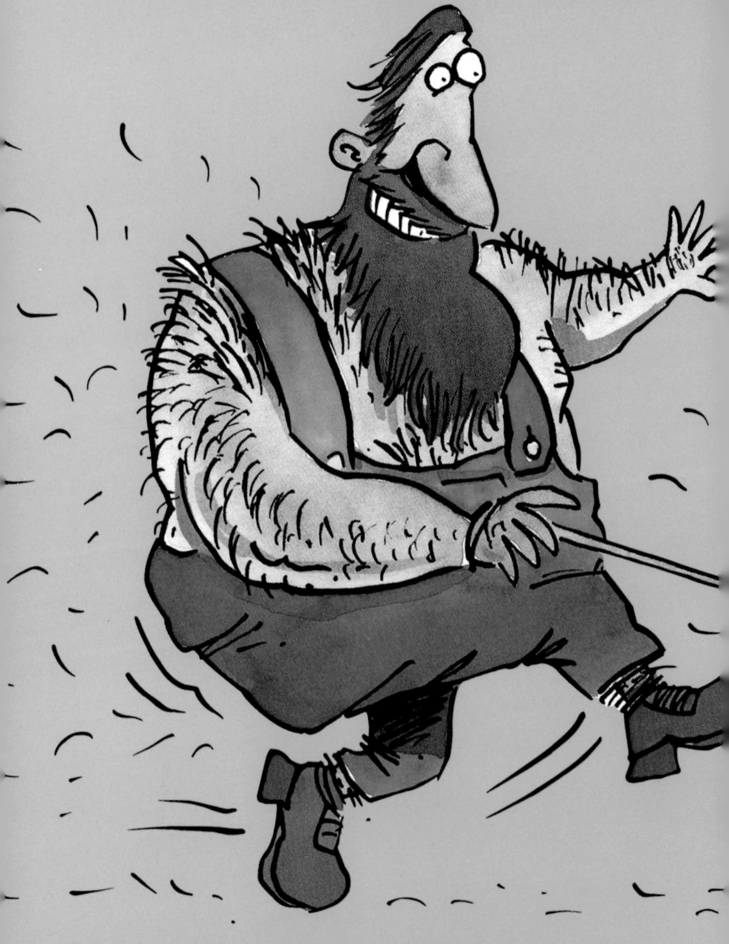

Too hairy

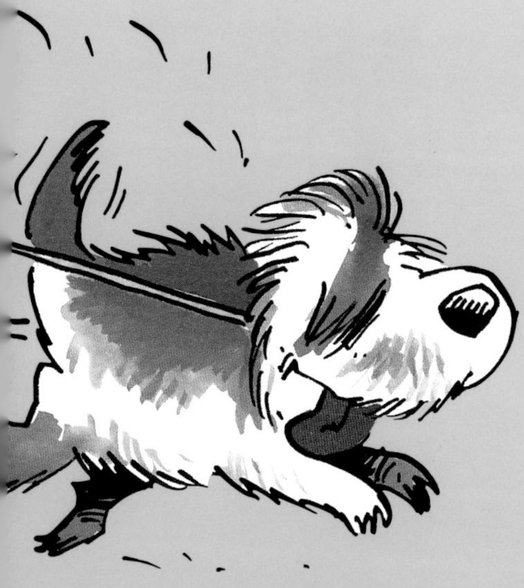

. . . far too embarrassing

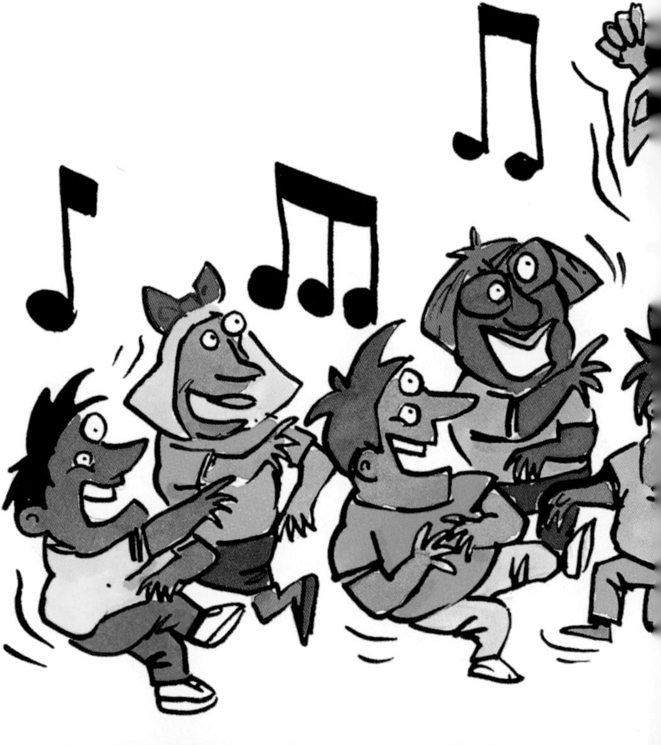

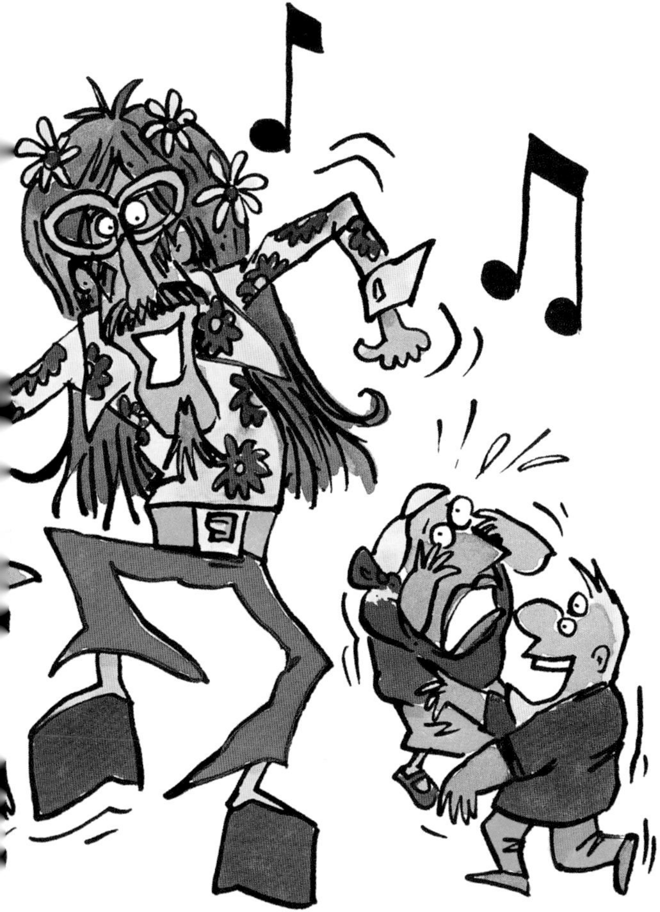

Just right!

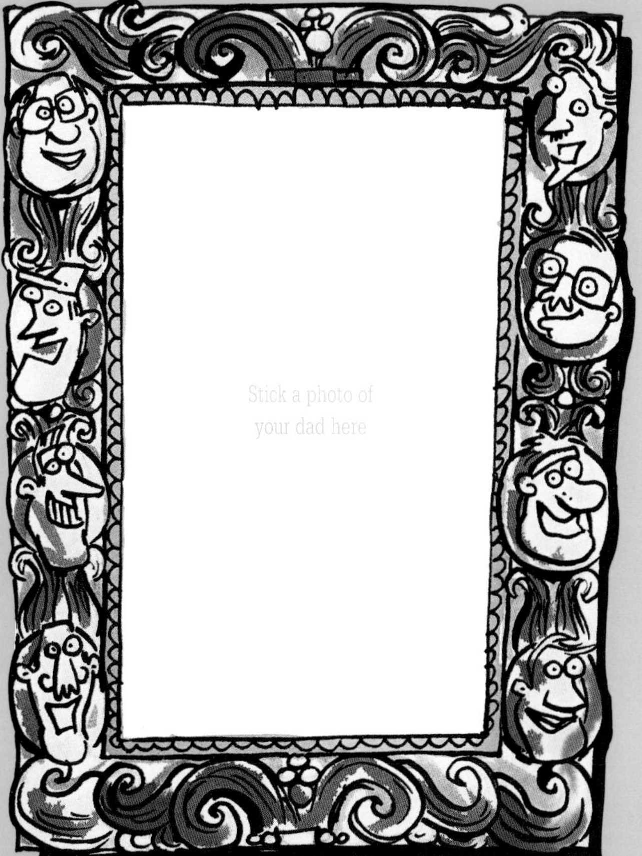
Stick a photo of
your dad here

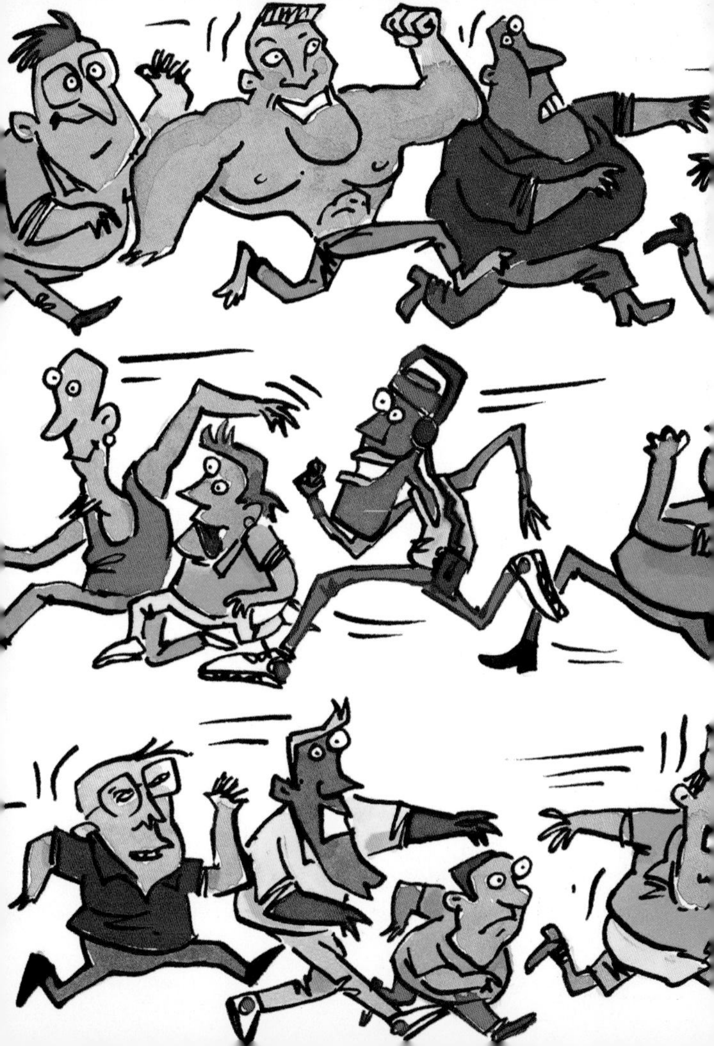